Puffin Books

The Second Young Puffin

Be a mastermind with this fun and informative quiz book. Test your knowledge on a wide range of subjects. There are fascinating questions on everything from castles to space, from the sea to food and drink. Whatever your interests, there are bound to be questions that you can answer, but which your friends can't. And you'll learn a lot from discovering the answers you don't know.

With its lively illustrations, this is an ideal sequel to Sally Kilroy's *Young Puffin Quiz Book*.

Sally Kilroy was brought up in south-west England. Following a course in Graphic Design at Canterbury College of Art, she went into the advertising business, working on such projects as the Smarties TV advertisements. Sally and her husband and two children now live near Weymouth, where she works from home on design projects and her books for children, of which she has written more than twenty.

The Second Young Puffin Quiz Book

Sally Kilroy

PUFFIN BOOKS

PUFFIN BOOKS

Published by the Penguin Group
Penguin Books Ltd, 27 Wrights Lane, London W8 5TZ, England
Penguin Books USA Inc., 375 Hudson Street, New York, New York 10014, USA
Penguin Books Australia Ltd, Ringwood, Victoria, Australia
Penguin Books Canada Ltd, 10 Alcorn Avenue, Toronto, Ontario, Canada M4V 3B2
Penguin Books (NZ) Ltd, 182–190 Wairau Road, Auckland 10, New Zealand

Penguin Books Ltd, Registered Offices: Harmondsworth, Middlesex, England

First published 1992
10 9 8 7 6 5 4 3 2 1

Text and illustrations copyright © Sally Kilroy, 1992
All rights reserved

The moral right of the author/illustrator has been asserted

Filmset in Helvetica
Printed in England by Clays Ltd, St Ives plc

For Ben, Naomi, Oliver, Sam,
Jim, Alice, Luke and Hermione

Castles

What did people in castle times eat?

a) hamburgers and chips
b) bread, cheese and meat
c) spaghetti bolognaise

What was a minstrel?

a) a travelling singer
b) the castle cook
c) a dog owned by a knight

What did they use for lights in early castles?

a) gas lanterns
b) oil-lamps
c) burning bundles of twigs or rushes

What is shooting an arrow at a target called?

a) archery
b) shooting
c) casting

What was a tournament?

a) a match on the castle tennis-court
b) a contest between two knights
c) an evening of singing and dancing

What is the strip of water around
some castles called?

a) the lake
b) the bailey
c) the moat

SNIFF!

7

What is the shaped top of a castle wall called?

a) the ridges
b) the battlements
c) the cornerstones

What did attackers use to try to make a hole in the castle walls?

a) tanks
b) catapults
c) charging horses

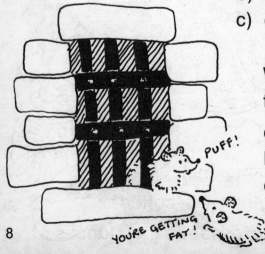

What was kept in the dungeons?

a) food supplies
b) prisoners
c) water

What is a coat of arms?

a) special arrow-proof paint for the gate
b) a suit of armour
c) a shield with the family's design on it

Which bird did noblemen take out to hunt with?

a) a hawk
b) a magpie
c) an eagle

What were the poles that knights charged each other with called?

a) spears b) crossbows c) lances

Animals

What do parrots eat?
a) fruit
b) fish
c) small animals

How does an octopus
confuse its enemies?

a) by cuddling them in its arms
b) by staring at them
c) by squirting ink at them

What is this animal?
a) a hippopotamus   b) a wild boar

c) a rhinoceros

Why does a camel
have spread-out feet?

a) because it is
   overweight
b) so it doesn't sink
   into the sand
c) because it is
   related to the duck

How many eyes do
most spiders have?

a) two   b) six   c) eight

Which of these
animals would
you not find in a
rain forest?

a) a snake
b) a monkey
c) a bear

11

WHEE!

Which has a tail –
a monkey or an
ape?

Which of these
birds is pink?

a) a stork
b) a peacock
c) a flamingo

What do cats use to
comb their fur?

a) their tongue
b) their paws
c) their teeth

12   Can all birds fly?

What is a group of
lions called?

a) a pride
b) a gang
c) a flock

An owl can turn its
head right round
and look backwards
– true or false?

ZOOM!

Which is the fastest
big cat?

a) the jaguar   b) the leopard
c) the cheetah

What is the shape
that a snail's shell
makes?

13

Humans get two new sets of teeth. How many sets do elephants get?

a) two
b) five
c) ten

What are baby seals called?

a) pups
b) calves
c) kids

Some animals go to sleep for the winter. What is this called?

a) a siesta
b) hibernation
c) a catnap

How do eagles
catch their prey?

a) by knocking them over
b) by grabbing them with their beaks
c) by swooping down and picking them
   up with their claws (talons)

Some snakes eat
small animals like
rats and mice – do
they bite them up
or eat them whole?

What is this
animal?

a) a sea lion
b) a walrus
c) an otter

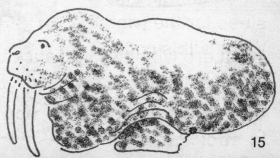

Buildings

What is cooked to make bricks and tiles?

a) clay
b) flour and water paste
c) earth and glue

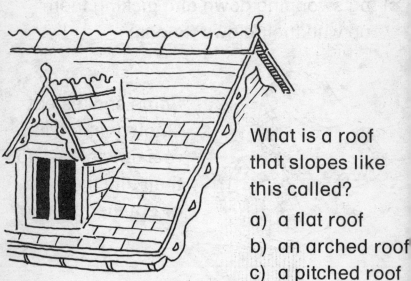

What is a roof that slopes like this called?

a) a flat roof
b) an arched roof
c) a pitched roof

What are windows that stick out of a sloping roof called?

a) dormer windows b) bow windows
c) roof lights

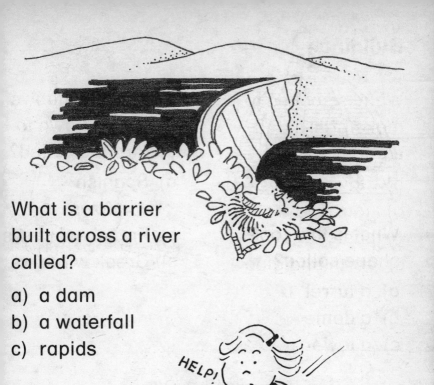

What is a barrier built across a river called?

a) a dam
b) a waterfall
c) rapids

What is a moving staircase called?

a) a spiral staircase
b) an escalator
c) a lift

17

What is this roof-shape called?

a) a turret
b) a dome
c) a tower

What are windows that open down to the ground called?

a) Spanish windows
b) French windows
c) Greek windows

WOW!

What sort of bridge is hung by cables from tall towers?

a) a tower bridge
b) a drawbridge
c) a suspension bridge

Where are aircraft kept?

a) a garage
b) a hangar
c) a conservatory

What were windmills used for?

a) making cheese
b) grinding corn
c) mixing paint

What is a very big church called?

a) a town hall
b) a courtroom
c) a cathedral

19

In town

AARGH!

Where would someone be taken who was badly hurt?

a) the fire station
b) the optician
c) the hospital

Where would you go to post a parcel?

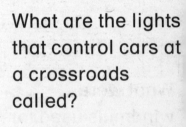

What are the lights that control cars at a crossroads called?

What are the underground pipes that carry waste water from a house called?

a) tunnels
b) sewers
c) tubes

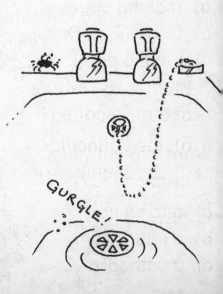

GURGLE!

What is a museum?

a) a place that sells pet food
b) somewhere you can borrow books
c) a place showing things from the past

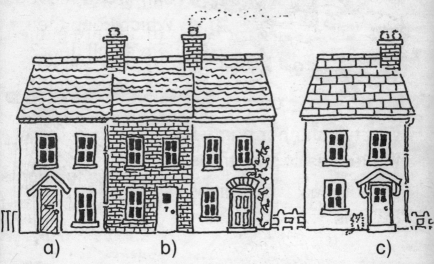

a)   b)   c)

Which house is terraced, which
semi-detached and which detached?

What is the leader
of a town called?

a) the councillor
b) the Member of
   Parliament
c) the Mayor

Trees

There are two kinds of tree – coniferous and broad-leaved. Which keep their leaves all year?

What is another name for the leaves of pine trees?

a) needles   b) spikes
c) pins

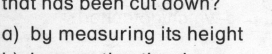

How can you tell the age of a tree that has been cut down?

a) by measuring its height
b) by counting the rings on the stump
c) by measuring round its trunk

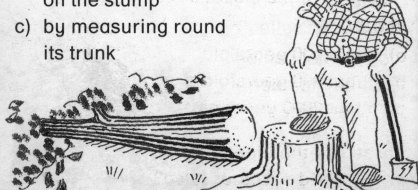

Which leaves belong
to which trees?
Willow, plane, oak

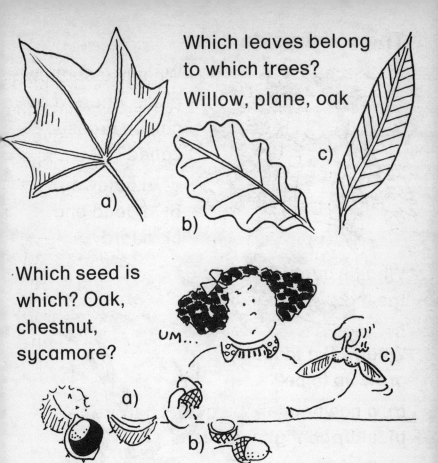

c)

b)

a)

Which seed is
which? Oak,
chestnut,
sycamore?

UM...

a)

b)

c)

How old are the oldest trees
in Britain?

a) about 100 years old
b) about 300 years old
c) about 2000 years old

These are the oldest trees
in the world – true or false?

The countryside

What is a shallow place where a river can be crossed called?

a) a gateway
b) a dead end
c) a ford

What will a tadpole grow up to be?

a) a newt
b) a dragonfly
c) a frog

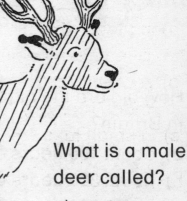

What is a male deer called?

a) a stag
b) a bull
c) a boar

What is a reservoir?

a) a viewpoint on an animal reserve
b) a place where water is stored
c) a group of fir trees being grown for flagpoles

What do horses that pull carts wear?

a) a yoke
b) a coat of arms
c) a harness

CLIP! CLOP!

What is a canal?

a) a place where rivers join the sea
b) a waterway made by man
c) a small lake

Which plant might you see a lot of on moorland?

a) heather
b) bluebells
c) geraniums

Do rivers flow from the mountains to the sea, or from the sea to the mountains?

Who makes metal shoes for horses' feet?

a) a shoemaker
b) a riding instructor
c) a blacksmith

What is a stile?

a) a small waterfall
b) an animal shelter
c) a place where people can cross a fence or hedge

What is a sheep's yearly haircut called?

a) combining
b) shearing
c) branding

About how many types of wild flower are there in Britain?

a) 17
b) 204
c) 1300

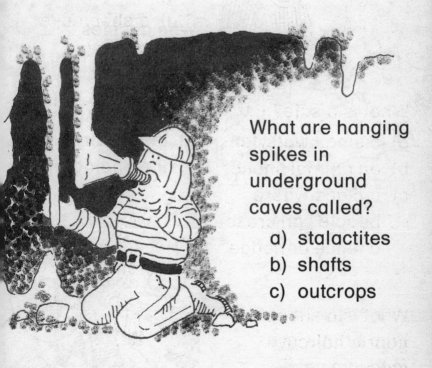

What are hanging spikes in underground caves called?

a) stalactites
b) shafts
c) outcrops

What is exploring underground caves or passages called?

a) tunnelling   b) mining   c) pot-holing

Jobs

Who plays sport
as a job rather
than a hobby –
a professional or
an amateur?

Who decides
what goes in the
newspaper?

a) the reporter
b) the editor
c) the photographer

Who brings you
food in a café?

a) a steward
b) a housekeeper
c) a waiter

What is a
policeman who
solves crimes
called?

a) a patrolman
b) a detective
c) a sergeant

What do police
sometimes use to
help them catch
criminals?

a) cats
b) dogs
c) ferrets

Who writes books?

a) an author
b) a librarian
c) a secretary

What does a
plumber do?

a) fixes lights and
cookers
b) fixes doors and
windows
c) fixes baths and
radiators

What does a sweep do?

a) sweeps up leaves in parks
b) cleans chimneys
c) collects winners' tickets
at a horse-race

Who would design
a bridge?

a) an engineer
b) a cabinet-maker
c) a chemist

Who stops all the
planes in the air
from crashing into
each other?

a) airport police
b) customs officers
c) air traffic controllers

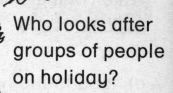

Who looks after
groups of people
on holiday?

a) a navigator
b) a hostess
c) a courier

What does a vet
look after?

a) your teeth
b) telephones
c) sick animals

NOTES

Food and drink

Which bird is eaten by many families at Christmas?

a) a swan
b) a turkey
c) an eagle

Which of these is not a sausage dish?

a) toad-in-the-hole
b) cat's whiskers
c) hot dog

What is wine usually made from?

a) greengages
b) grapes
c) gooseberries

What is a pavlova?

a) a Russian soup
b) a meringue and fruit pudding
c) a lamb stew

Which country does
sherry come from?

a) Scotland
b) France
c) Spain

Which animals
do we need to
make cheese?

a) cows
b) bees
c) pigs

33

In France frog's legs are a special treat to eat – true or false?

What is an omelette made from?
a) chicken rolled in breadcrumbs
b) minced beef
c) beaten eggs

When do you eat hot cross buns?
a) at Christmas
b) at Easter
c) on bonfire night

Which of these berries should you not eat?

raspberry   hollyberry
blueberry   blackberry
gooseberry

Bananas are green when they are picked – true or false?

What is marmalade made from?

a) Seville oranges
b) kiwi fruit
c) morello cherries

Which of these grows in water?

a) spaghetti
b) potatoes
c) rice

Music

Which of these instruments is associated with Scotland?

a) the cello
b) the organ
c) the bagpipes

What is an orchestra?

a) a choir of male and female singers
b) a group of people playing instruments
c) a tribal war-dance

Which of these was not a famous composer?

Bach
Mozart
Picasso
Beethoven

TUM TE TUM!

What instruments do angels often carry?

a) guitars
b) harps
c) drums

What are the wooden clappers that Spanish ladies dance with called?

a) castanets
b) cymbals
c) maracas

How many notes or keys does a piano have?

a) 60   b) 88   c) 124

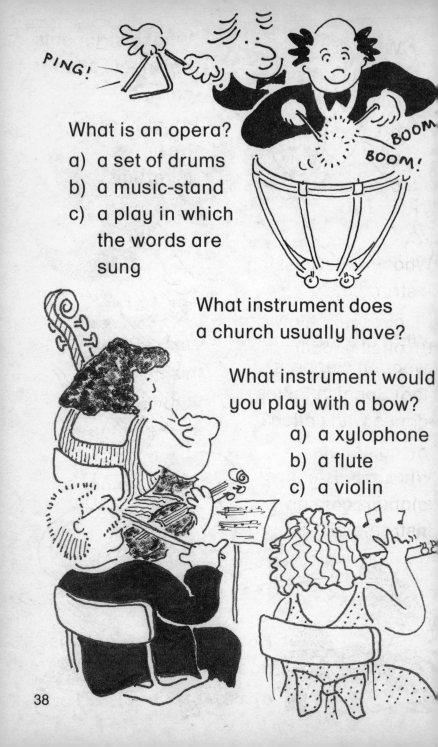

PING!

What is an opera?

a) a set of drums
b) a music-stand
c) a play in which the words are sung

BOOM BOOM!

What instrument does a church usually have?

What instrument would you play with a bow?

a) a xylophone
b) a flute
c) a violin

What is a
conductor's stick
called?

a) a bow
b) a cymbal
c) a baton

What are percussion
instruments?

a) ones you blow down
b) ones you hit
c) ones you pluck
the strings of

What instrument is
this person
playing?

a) the trumpet
b) the tuba
c) the trombone

What mathematical
shape is also an
instrument?

People and places

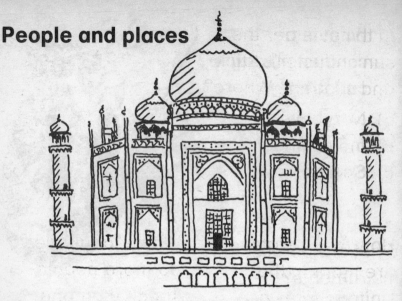

The Taj Mahal is one of the most beautiful buildings in the world. Where is it?

In which country are Maoris the native people?

a) Switzerland
b) Poland
c) New Zealand

Which country is the Amazon river in?

a) Brazil
b) Italy
c) Argentina

In the summer the sun shines all day and all night. Where?

a) Norway
b) India
c) Spain

PHEW!

How many states are there in the United States of America?

a) 50
b) 37
c) 21

Which language do more people speak than any other?

a) English
b) Chinese
c) French

What might you ride in on a canal in Venice?

a) a punt   b) a gondola   c) a cruiser   41

What is this famous building in Australia called?

a) the Brisbane Museum
b) the Wellington Town Hall
c) the Sydney Opera House

Where did the Romans come from?

a) Italy
b) Spain
c) Germany

What is the most famous place where films are made called?

a) San Francisco
b) Montreal
c) Hollywood

In which country would you find cowboys and Indians?

a) Sweden
b) America
c) Africa

What do cowboys catch cattle with?

a) a tomahawk
b) a lasso
c) a rodeo

Where do most diamonds come from?

a) South America
b) South Africa   c) Japan

Where is there a famous tower that leans?

a) London
b) Moscow   c) Pisa

Gadgets

What is this and
what is it for?

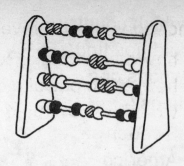

What shows you which way north is?

a) a metronome   b) a compass
c) a battery

What can police
fasten people's
hands together
with?

a) a clamp
b) a bicycle lock
c) handcuffs

What do people use
to study the stars?

a) binoculars
b) an eyeglass
c) a telescope

What does a spirit level measure?

a) how much whisky someone has drunk
b) how much petrol a car has in it
c) whether something is level

What can time people exactly in a race?

a) a digital watch
b) a stop-watch
c) a 24-hour clock

What is this called?

What does it tell us?

a) it points to the nearest town
b) nothing – it's just decoration
c) it shows where the wind is blowing from

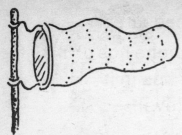

What shows us how hot or cold it is?

a) a barometer
b) a thermometer
c) a rain-gauge

What shows which way the wind is blowing at a small airport?

a) a wind-sock
b) a kite
c) an air balloon

What is used in Chinese cooking to fry food over a high heat?

a) a microwave
b) a pressure cooker
c) a wok

What would you keep a pet fish in?

a) a solarium
b) an aquarium
c) a jacuzzi

What is used to
open a wine bottle?

a) a bottle opener
b) a wine cooler
c) a corkscrew

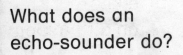

What does an
echo-sounder do?

a) tells ships how deep
the water is below them
b) warns trains in tunnels that
another is coming
c) tests if people at the back of a
meeting can hear all right

What can add up
figures for us?

a) a generator
b) a refrigerator
c) a calculator

What would you
take a photograph
with?

The sea

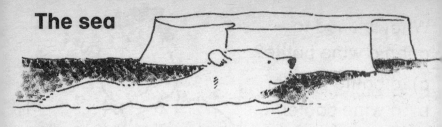

What are large lumps
of floating ice called?

a) icicles   b) ice-cubes   c) icebergs

What is someone
who hides on a
ship to get a free
ride called?

a) a cabin boy
b) a deck-hand
c) a stowaway

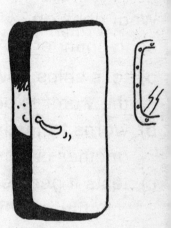

Where do you
sleep on a ship?

a) in a galley
b) in a cabin
c) in a
   companionway

What sort of diving is done with an aqualung (tanks of air)?

a) scuba diving
b) snorkelling
c) skydiving

What do divers wear on their feet?

What can divers get after they have been in deep water?

a) blue toes
b) the bends
c) a cold

Which is bigger – a shrimp or a prawn?

WOW!

What is the big
bulging sail at the
front of a sailing-
boat called?

a) a mainsail
b) a spinnaker
c) a jib

SPLUTTER!

What is it called
when a sailing-
boat tips over?

a) going about
b) tacking
c) capsizing

What should people
who go out in small
boats wear?

a) a waistcoat
b) a life-jacket
c) a duffle coat

Who could come on
board and guide a
ship into port?

a) a coastguard
b) a harbour-master
c) a pilot

What are the most used
routes across the sea called?

a) the deep channels
b) the shipping lanes
c) the long passages

What makes the
tides happen?

a) the moon
b) the wind
c) moving ships

How many times a
day do you get a high
tide and a low tide?

a) once
b) twice
c) four times

51

Sport

What game is played with a racket and a tiny black ball?

a) snooker
b) badminton
c) squash

Who wears shoes with studs on the bottom?

a) a footballer
b) a cyclist
c) a tennis player

What are the three upright sticks behind the batsman in cricket called?

a) clubs
b) stumps
c) goal-posts

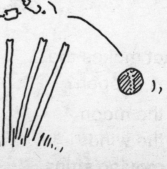

What colour are the first, second and third Olympic medals?

WOW!

What is the game played by people on horses, hitting a ball with a stick called?

a) athletics
b) hockey
c) polo

In which sport do you use an iron?

Who keeps order in
a football match?

a) an umpire   b) a coach
c) a referee

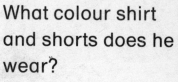

What colour shirt
and shorts does he
wear?

a) dark blue
b) white
c) black

How long is the
London Marathon?

a) 17 miles
b) 26 miles
c) 40 miles

If you hit the middle
of a target, you
score a . . .

a) pig's nose
b) flea's ear
c) bull's-eye

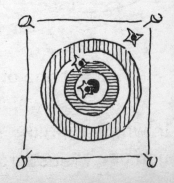

What is the sport
of sword-fighting
called?

a) fencing
b) jousting
c) sprinting

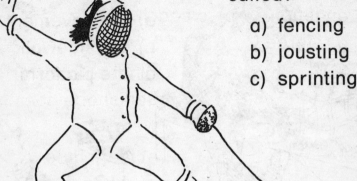

What does a cox do?

a) keeps score in a cricket match
b) keeps a rowing-team in time
c) teaches gymnastics

All but one of these are swimming
strokes: which is the odd one out?

backstroke   crawl   quickstep

breaststroke   butterfly

Transport

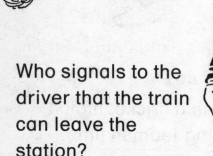

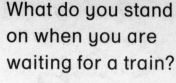

What do you stand on when you are waiting for a train?

a) the pavement
b) the sidewalk
c) the platform

Who signals to the driver that the train can leave the station?

a) the porter
b) the guard
c) the station-master

What are the pads on the front of an engine and at the end of a railway line called?

a) bumpers   b) buffers   c) brake pads

What are the white lines that planes
sometimes leave in the sky called?

a) flight paths   b) vapour trails
c) runways

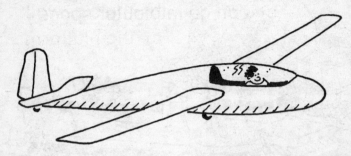

Which aircraft has
no engine?

a) a jump-jet
b) a helicopter
c) a glider

Which side of the
road do cars drive
on in . . . ?

a) England
b) France
c) America

Concorde is a supersonic plane.
What does supersonic mean?
a) flies upside down
b) travels faster than sound
c) can go into outer space

A hovercraft travels on a cushion of –
a) water   b) gas   c) air

What is this person using?
a) a jet-ski   b) a windsurfer
c) a canoe

What was the space
shuttle that blew up called?

a) Challenger   b) Defender   c) Victory

What is a juggernaut?

a) a mechanical digger
b) a large articulated lorry
c) a crane

This sailing-boat is used in countries
like China. What is it called?

a) a junk   b) a barge
c) a paddle-steamer

The body

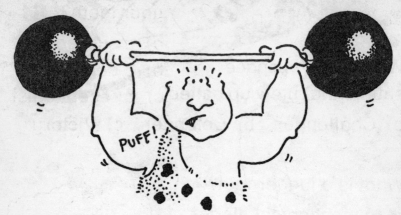

How many bones does a human have?

a) 27
b) 124
c) 206

What gives us the strength to lift something heavy?

a) kidneys
b) muscles
c) lungs

What do babies need most?

a) fruit purée
b) milk
c) lemonade

Who looks after your teeth?

a) a surgeon
b) a dentist
c) a receptionist

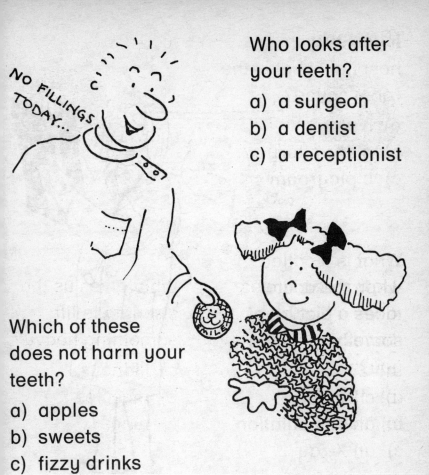

Which of these does not harm your teeth?

a) apples
b) sweets
c) fizzy drinks

How many teeth do babies normally have when they are born?

a) 4
b) 2
c) 0

If you stay in hospital, what is the room called?

a) a ward
b) a dormitory
c) a playroom

What is it called when the doctor takes a picture of something inside you?

a) a fracture
b) an innoculation
c) an X-ray

If you are ill your temperature goes up. What is it normally?

a) 37 (98.6)
b) 39 (102)
c) 40 (104)

If you break your leg, what would it be put in?

a) a sling
b) a bandage
c) plaster

What does a doctor listen to your breathing with?

a) a thermometer
b) a stethoscope
c) an ear-trumpet

If you need an operation, what are you given to make you sleepy?

a) a glucose sweet
b) an anaesthetic
c) a blood test

63

Space

What happens to liquid in space?

a) it freezes
b) it pours upside down
c) if floats about in tiny drops

What is a laser?

a) a beam of light
b) a gas-filled rocket
c) a cartridge of explosives

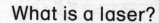

What is the thick layer of air around the earth called?

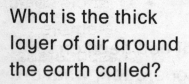

a) the galaxy
b) the planet
c) the atmosphere

Where do people control a space flight from on earth?

a) a satellite
b) a space station
c) mission control

Some things can be made more easily in space conditions – true or false?

What might battle stations in space be able to fire to destroy missiles sent from one country to another?

a) lasers
b) supersonic fighters
c) spacelabs

An American unmanned spacecraft has been to Mars. Did it find any sign of life?

Entertainment

What is it called when you act in silence?

a) judo
b) mime
c) prompting

What sort of dancers wear shoes with metal plates under the toe and heel?

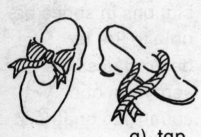

a) tap   b) ballroom   c) folk

What is a film that is made from lots of painted pictures called?

a) a feature
b) a cartoon
c) a documentary

What would you expect to see in a theatre?

a) a cricket match
b) a game of snooker
c) a play

What can you speak or sing into to make your voice louder?

a) a microwave
b) a microphone
c) a microlite

I CAN'T SEE

What is the person who works out dancers' steps called?

a) the conductor
b) the producer
c) the choreographer

What are the people watching a performance called?

a) the audience
b) the chorus
c) the orchestra

The weather

What is a long time
without rain called?

a) a drought
b) a monsoon
c) a desert

Does the moon
glow because . . . ?

a) it is burning like the sun
b) it reflects the sun
c) its rocks are luminous

What are clouds
made of?

a) white smoke
b) tiny drops of water
c) fine strands of
fluff

In Australia Christmas is in
the summer – true or false?

How many points does
a snowflake have?

a) none – they are round
b) six
c) eight

It is thought that the
earth's atmosphere
may be getting hotter –
what is this called?

a) solar panelling
b) global warming
c) central heating

Which would you
see or hear first –
lightning or
thunder?

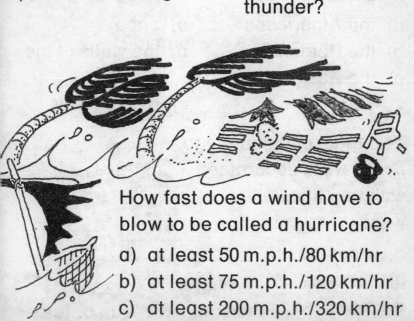

How fast does a wind have to
blow to be called a hurricane?

a) at least 50 m.p.h./80 km/hr
b) at least 75 m.p.h./120 km/hr
c) at least 200 m.p.h./320 km/hr

The past

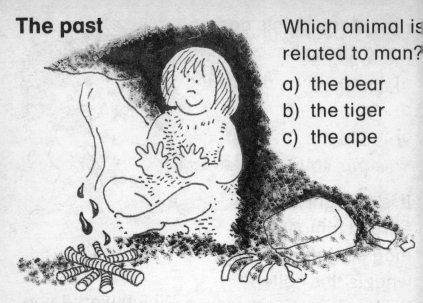

Which animal is related to man?

a) the bear
b) the tiger
c) the ape

Which ancient people was famous for building roads?

a) the Americans
b) the Romans
c) the Australians

Long ago people lived in caves. What did they draw on?

a) paper
b) the walls of the cave
c) blackboards

Two thousand years ago floors were decorated with tiny tiles. What were these called?

a) tapestries
b) collages
c) mosaics

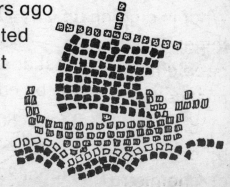

Before people had money, they exchanged goods of equal value. What was this called?

a) catering
b) banking
c) bartering

In which country were kings buried under huge stone pyramids?

a) Egypt   b) Canada
c) Spain

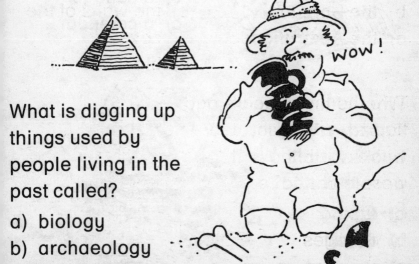

What is digging up things used by people living in the past called?

a) biology
b) archaeology
c) chemistry

General knowledge

What do you use to write on a blackboard?

a) wax crayons
b) pencils
c) chalk

What is a picture made out of lots of bits of paper called?

a) a patchwork
b) a collage
c) a calendar

What is the special raised writing in books for blind people called?

a) typing
b) Braille
c) lip-reading

Nearly one third of the people in the world over 15 cannot read and write – true or false?

What are pottery objects made of?

a) chalk
b) flour and water
c) clay

When the height of a mountain is marked on a map, is it from the bottom of it or from sea-level?

Where does the
Pope live?

a) Vatican City
b) Mexico City
c) Salt Lake City

What is the hardest
thing in the world?

a) steel
b) diamonds
c) concrete

Sometimes you can
find the remains of
prehistoric animals
or plants in the
ground. What are
these called?

a) crystals
b) chippings
c) fossils

What is the part of
spectacles that you
look through
called?

a) the lens
b) the pupils
c) the glasses

What is it called
each time a racing
car goes round the
track?

a) a circuit
b) a trip
c) a lap

What are corks
made from?

a) the bark of a tree
b) underwater
   sponges
c) pressed sawdust

What are fertilizers?

a) fizzy drinks
b) something used by farmers to
   give better crops
c) exercises to make you slimmer

Can seaweed
live in any
depth of water?

Answers

Castles (pages 6–9)

Bread, cheese and meat; a travelling singer;
burning bundles of twigs or rushes; archery; a
contest between two knights; the moat; the
battlements; catapults – huge ones firing stones;
prisoners; a shield with the family's design on
it; a hawk; lances

Animals (pages 10–15)

Fruit; by squirting ink at them; a rhinoceros; so
it doesn't sink into the sand; eight, arranged in
two rows of four; a bear; a monkey; a flamingo;
their tongue, which is covered in tiny hooks; no
– birds like ostriches and penguins can't; a pride;
true; the cheetah – most big cats pounce on
their prey, but the cheetah is fast enough to
chase and kill it; a spiral; five; pups; hibernation;
by swooping down and picking them up with
their claws (talons); they eat them whole; a
walrus

Buildings (pages 16–19)

Clay; a pitched roof; dormer windows; a dam –
it controls the flow of water; an escalator;
French windows; a dome; a suspension bridge;
a hangar; grinding corn; a cathedral

In town (pages 20–21)

The hospital; the post office; traffic lights;
sewers; a place showing things from the past;
a) is semi-detached, b) terraced and c) detached;
the Mayor

Trees (pages 22–23)

Coniferous trees – although a few broad-leaved trees like holly do too; needles; by counting the rings on the stump; a) plane b) oak c) willow; a) chestnut b) oak c) sycamore; some yew trees are about 2000 years old; false – some bristle-pine trees in the USA are at least 4900 years old!

The countryside (pages 24–27)

A ford; a frog; a stag; a place where water is stored; a harness; a waterway made by man; heather; from the mountains to the sea; a blacksmith; a place where people can cross a fence or hedge; shearing; 1300; stalactites; pot-holing

Jobs (pages 28–31)

A professional; the editor; a waiter (or waitress); a detective; dogs; an author; fixes baths and radiators; cleans chimneys; an engineer; air traffic controllers; a courier; sick animals

Food and drink (pages 32–35)

A turkey; cat's whiskers; grapes; a meringue and fruit pudding; Spain; cows, because cheese is made from milk – it can be made from goat's or sheep's milk too; true; beaten eggs; at Easter; hollyberry; true; Seville oranges; rice

Music (pages 36–39)

The bagpipes; a group of people playing instruments; Picasso was a famous painter; harps; castanets; 88; a play in which the words are sung; an organ; a violin; a baton; ones you hit; a triangle; the trombone

People and places (pages 40–43)

India; New Zealand; Brazil; in Northern Norway; 50–48 together, plus Alaska and the island of Hawaii; Chinese (more people live in China than in any other country); a gondola; the Sydney Opera House; Italy; Hollywood; America; a lasso; South Africa; Pisa, Italy

Gadgets (pages 44–47)

An abacus, which can help you add up; a compass; handcuffs; a telescope; whether something is level; a stop-watch; a weathercock; it shows where the wind is blowing from; a thermometer; a wind-sock; a wok; an aquarium; a corkscrew; it tells ships how deep the water is below them – by measuring how long a noise takes to bounce back; a calculator; a camera

The sea (pages 48–51)

Icebergs; a stowaway; in a cabin; scuba diving; flippers; the bends; a prawn; a spinnaker; capsizing; a life-jacket; a pilot; the shipping lanes; the moon – it pulls the water towards it, and because the earth is spinning, another bulge appears on the opposite side; twice

Sport (pages 52–55)

Squash; a footballer; stumps – two small bails sit on top; gold, silver and bronze; polo; golf; a referee; black; 26 miles; bull's-eye; fencing; keeps a rowing-team in time; quickstep is a

dance

Transport (pages 56–59)

The platform; the guard; buffers; vapour trails; left, right, right; a glider; travels faster than sound; air; a jet-ski; Challenger; a large articulated lorry; a junk

The body (pages 60–63)

206; muscles; milk; a dentist; apples; 0; a ward; an X-ray; 37 (98.6); plaster; a stethoscope; an anaesthetic

Space (pages 64–65)

It floats about in tiny drops – so it must be drunk from a container through a straw; a beam of light – these can be powerful enough to destroy metal; the atmosphere; mission control; true – there may be a silicon-chip factory in space one day; lasers; no

Entertainment (pages 66–67)

Mime; tap; a cartoon; a play; a microphone; the choreographer; the audience

The weather (pages 68–69)

A drought; it reflects the sun; tiny drops of water; true – countries on the southern side of the world have summer at Christmas; six – although the patterns are always different; global warming; lightning – because light travels faster than sound; at least 75 m.p.h./120 km/hr

The past (pages 70–71)

The ape; the Romans; the walls of the cave; mosaics; bartering; Egypt; archaeology

General knowledge (pages 72–75)

Chalk; a collage; Braille; true; clay; from sea-level; Vatican City, which is an independent country in the middle of Rome; diamonds; fossils; the lens; a lap; the bark of a tree; something used by farmers to give better crops; no – only in shallow water because it needs sunlight to make food